M000083615

TRANSPARENT
TAPE

*Over **350** Super, Simple and*

Surprising Uses

You've Probably Never Thought of

by

Vicki Lansky

second edition

illustrations by Martha Campbell

distributed to the book trade by
Publishers Group West, Berkeley, CA

BOOK PEDDLERS
Minnetonka, MN

Special thanks to:
Abby Rabinovitz, Francie Paper, Kathryn Ring, Cindy Shellum,
Linda Fay and 3M Consumer Stationery Division

ISBN: 1-931863-32-6
NEW ISBN 13: 978-1931863-32-2

Publisher's Cataloging in Publication
(Prepared by Quality Books Inc.)

LANSKY, VICKI.
Transparent tape : over 350 super, simple and surprising uses
you've probably never thought of : by Vicki Lansky ; illustrations
by Martha Campbell.
p. cm.
Includes index.
ISBN 1-931863-32-6

1. Home economics--Miscellanea. 2. Adhesive tape--Miscellanea.
I. Campbell, Martha, ill. II. Title.

TX158.L367 1995   640'.41
                            QB195-20108

Book Peddlers
2828 Hedberg Drive, Minnetonka, MN 55305
952-544-1154
www.bookpeddlers.com • info@bookpeddlers.com

07 08 09   5 4 3

TABLE OF CONTENTS

Dear Reader,

I don't remember when I first used transparent tape. It was one of those things that was always there. Or so it seemed. Like electricity, the telephone and cars. There are so many aids to our daily life that we take for granted and transparent tape is definitely one of them.

As my career as an author, collector and columnist of tips grew, so did my file of uses for transparent tape. That's what I'm sharing with you now. No, I haven't used tape in every way mentioned here, but someone has. That's how I came to hear about these ideas. I suspect you'll find many that will be useful for you. Use your common sense. I cannot guarantee the use of all the ideas you'll find here, but I know you're going to find a lot of good ones—even some funny ones—that you can use to make your life a bit easier or more cost-efficient.

The folks at 3M, tape makers since 1930, have been kind enough to provide me with information and feedback, but this book has not been written for them. Though they are enthusiastic about the book, they are not responsible for the information printed here.

Did I miss one of your favorite uses? Please let me know. You can e-mail me at vlansky@bookpeddlers.com or write to me in care of the publisher.

Enjoy!

Vicki Lansky

PS. You will see the abbreviation—SSO—used throughout the book. It stands for STICKY SIDE OUT. SSO is when you create a loop of the tape so it sticks to itself and the adhesive side faces "out." This allows it to be used in many additional ways—as you will see.

TRANSPARENT TAPE

HOW IT CAME TO BE

AND

HOW IT CAME TO BE SO SUCCESSFUL

Is there anyone not familiar with transparent tape and at least some of its uses? Transparent tape can be found in homes and offices around the world today. How did it get to be such a popular, ubiquitous part of our lives? The wide- spread use of what appears to be a simple product, took a curious man named Richard Drew years to develop and perfect. This process, started to meet an industrial need, created a household staple.

THE ACCIDENTAL INVENTOR

At the age of 21, Richard Drew a young laboratory technician worked his way through college playing banjo in dance bands. He dropped out of school in 1920 and took an engineering correspondence course. In 1921 he answered a blind ad for a lab technician at 3M (which was then known as Minnesota Mining and Manufacturing) to assist in quality control at its research laboratory.

Back then, 3M was a struggling sandpaper manufacturer. Drew spent his first two years at 3M checking raw materials and running tests for products in development. In 1923, 3M developed the first waterproof sandpaper. Drew was asked to take trial batches of the new sandpaper to a local auto body shop for testing. Two-tone paint finishes on cars had just been introduced and had become the rage. Auto manufacturers discovered that they had created a monstrous hassle for themselves. During the spray-painting of the cars, there was no effective way to keep one color masked from the other when painting a straight line. How could they mask the first paint without lifting the paint off with it? Painters would improvise with newspapers, butcher paper, various glues, surgical adhesive tape and other unsuitable products. That day in the auto body shop, Drew watched as the painter removed gummed kraft paper from a shining new Packard, stripping the paint away with it. Right then and there he decided that he would develop a tape to make two-tone paint application easier.

By coincidence, 3M management was searching for a way to diversify the company, and they gave Drew the time and financial backing to conduct some experiments on his tape idea. The young inventor's promise turned into two years of work. Seeking the perfect adhesive, Drew experimented with vegetable oils, various resins, chicle, linseed and glue glycerin. (Perhaps because of this initial research, Drew always called himself, even decades later, a "kitchen cook" rather than a chemist.) For the tape base, he finally settled on some left-over treated crepe paper. Drew brought samples of the new tape to the auto makers in Detroit and they immediately placed an order for three carloads. It was 1925 and masking tape was born. 3M, a sandpaper manufacturer in its twenty-third year, found itself in a new business—pressure-sensitive adhesives.

Five years later Drew conceived the product that would bring 3M worldwide fame. Like masking tape, this innovation was inspired by customer need. A Minnesota firm had an order to insulate hundreds of refrigerated railroad cars. There was a problem to be solved. The insulation would have to be protected from the moisture of the refrigeration. It could be wrapped in waterproof material, but the wrap would need a waterproof seal. The insulation firm consulted 3M. Richard Drew, now resident pressure-adhesives expert, began mulling over the challenge of inventing a waterproof tape.

In the meantime, while Drew was experimenting with new tape "recipes," Dupont came out with a revolutionary packaging material called cellophane. It was an immediate hit with food distributors because it was moisture proof. When another 3M researcher showed Drew the new filmy, transparent material, Drew had a flash of inspiration. Why not coat the stuff with adhesive? It was already waterproof. By the time Drew came up with a prototype, the insulation firm was no longer interested in waterproof tape, but many other companies were. The bakers, meat packers, confectioners, grocers and chewing gum manufacturers that had adopted cellophane food wrap were all calling for a moisture proof, attractive way to seal their packaging.

Even if the market was ready, the product was not. Moving the cellophane tape from prototype stage to salability took Drew and his colleagues a year. Using cellophane as a backing for adhesive, posed many difficulties. It curled near heat, split when machine coated and wouldn't take the adhesive evenly. At the end of each day a truck was needed to cart away the stacks of spoiled cellophane.

One by one, however, the 3M researchers solved the production problems. They discovered that if a primer coat was applied to the cellophane, the adhesive would hold evenly. They designed new coating machinery that protected the cellophane from splitting, and they stopped using the standard masking tape adhesive. Instead, they developed a new, almost colorless, adhesive to preserve the transparency of the cellophane.

TO MARKET, TO MARKET

On September 8, 1930, 3M sent the first trial shipment of this new cellulose tape to Shellmar Products Corporation, a Chicago firm specializing in the fancy printing of cellophane bakery wrap. Two weeks later, the delighted company wrote back, "Put this product on the market."

3M, however, still had its reservations. The new tape required many improvements. The company's 1930 annual report mentioned it only briefly: "During the year, a new product known as Scotch Cellulose Tape was introduced. It consists of cellophane coated with a transparent pressure-sensitive adhesive. Although it has many uses, its largest utility is sealing packages wrapped in moisture-proof cellophane. In view of the present popularity of cellophane as a wrapping medium, this market appears to have large possibilities."

Sales for that year were $33, and if that weren't unpromising enough, not long after the tape's introduction, the auto manufacturers invented a process for two-tone paint application. Scotch Cellulose Tape promptly became obsolete in the exact area for which it had been designed.

HOW "Scotch" STUCK FOR A NAME

The company's most famous "Scotch" brand trademark is believed to have had its origin with an angry auto body painter in the mid-1920's who was having trouble with the adhesion of an early roll of masking tape. Noticing that the two-inch-wide roll had adhesive only on its edges, he told a salesman, "Take this tape back to your stingy Scotch bosses and tell them to put more adhesive on it" or "Why be so 'Scotch' with the adhesive?" The story made the rounds in the office and may have sparked the inspiration for the name that became its trademark. Whether the first batch of tape stuck or not, the name certainly did. 3M's red, green and yellow tartan plaid design—a registered trademark—as a visual symbol was created by a package designer and introduced in the 1940's. It replaced the original blue and white packaging which had previously been used. Currently, 3M's transparent tape is identified by a red/black/yellow tartan plaid: their "Magic" invisible tape is identified by a green/black/yellow tartan plaid.

This setback ultimately didn't matter, because many food distributors and retailers continued to seal their packages with Scotch tape. In addition consumers of every description soon discovered the new waterproof transparent tape for themselves. They adapted it for uses its inventor had never imagined.

The Depression should have been the worst possible time to introduce a new product but because lack of money was forcing people to scrimp, conserve and refrain from purchases, it worked to 3M's advantage. Scotch cellulose tape was the answer to Americans' now overwhelming need to "make do." It enabled them to prolong the usefulness of old things. Homemakers used the new tape to seal opened cans of evaporated or condensed milk, attach labels to home-canned food, mend torn pages of books and fix broken toys. Insurance companies used it to repair torn policies, banks used it on torn currency, women mended their torn finger-nails with it and farmers used it on cracked turkey eggs! The new tape sold itself.

By World War II, the product had become such a ubiquitous part of American life that 3M felt compelled to run advertisements apologizing to homemakers for the scarcity of the tape in stores across the country because all available supplies had been designated for the war effort. 3M promised, "when victory comes, Scotch Cellulose Tape will be back in your home and office."

MAKING A GOOD IDEA BETTER

Over the years, 3M has made significant product improve-ments. For instance, originally one had to use a scissors to cut a piece of tape from the roll. The edge would stick back on the roll and was exasperating to find and peel off again. This product defect was solved by John Borden, a product sales manager. It took him 18 months of experimenting to design an efficient dispenser with a built-in cutter blade. The dispenser allowed the tape to be unwound, cut off and applied in seconds, keeping the new edge handy for the next application—the basic design is still used today.

Production and merchandising difficulties continued, however. The shelf life of the early tape was shortened by humidity, heat or cold. While the laboratory worked to overcome these difficulties, salesmen had to warn customers to keep the tape away from radiators and windows. In 1961, 3M engineers perfected the tape so that it would not yellow or ooze adhesive. Today's transparent tape is also treated to give one of its variations a matte surface that makes it virtually "invisible" when applied to most surfaces. Appearing frosty on the roll but invisible on the page, this improved tape was given the name Scotch Brand Magic tape. Today, 3M makes more than 100 types of pressure-sensitive tapes and more than 400 varieties are sold under the Scotch Brand label.

HOW IT'S MADE

The acetate film used for transparent tape today is a special type made from the raw material of wood pulp or cotton linters. Moisture is removed through a drying process, then a plasticized material much like oil is added to the processed raw material, resulting in small pieces of acetate plastic. This is melted or dissolved and formed into sheets about the thickness of a piece of paper. If it is to be used as "Magic" invisible tape, it is given a matte finish at this point. The film is then wound onto huge rolls ready to be coated with adhesive. Twenty-nine raw materials go into the production of the adhesives used. Ten separate steps are required to produce a single finished roll of transparent tape after the film and the adhesive have been produced. The simple roll of tape you have at home was not really that simple to make after all!

Invisible cellophane tape is a premium, higher priced product compared to regular transparent pressure sensitive tape.

OTHER TAPE MAKERS

One of the other major producers of transparent tape is LePage's, Inc., though it is probably best known for its uniquely shaped Mucilage glue bottle—tall and tapered with its angled rubber-tip dispenser. In 1956 LePage's started producing pressure sensitive tapes and continues to be a major producer of a large line of tapes, especially in the area of private label products. They manufacture for major retailers, contract stationery clients, industrial suppliers and government supply agencies.

ADHESIVE INNOVATION CONTINUES

The most recent example of today's innovative adhesive technology is seen in the Post-it™ product line introduced by 3M in May 1980. This is the note paper that has eliminated the need for pins, tacks and other fasteners. The note papers are coated on the back with a repositionable adhesive and can be used repeatedly before losing their adhesiveness. This permits notes to be stuck to almost anything temporarily and then reused as needed.

Many of the new advances in adhesive innovation today, such as the Post-it™ note, seem to be almost solely in competition with themselves…when using a Post-it™ note, you don't need a piece of tape to hold it in place. In 1993 3M introduced 167 totally new products and countless product extensions. One new type of Scotch tape apparently gets stronger the further it's stretched. And there is also Scotch Pop-up Tape.

The creation of transparent and invisible tape is a wonderful American business story. But equally wonderful are the numbers of inventive uses created by the people who like and use the product. I think even Richard Drew would be impressed with all these creative uses for transparent tape. And I think you will be, too.

CHAPTER ONE

AT HOME
- — IN THE KITCHEN
- — HOME LIFE
- — THE ELECTRONIC AGE
- — HOME MAINTENANCE
- — SUPER HANDY HINTS

IN THE KITCHEN

FOOD AIDS

- To check for ripeness in a melon, cut out a small triangle and taste. If it isn't ready, stick the triangle back in and criss-cross over the piece with tape until it is ripe.

- Secure small bundles of fresh herbs to your cutting board when chopping.

- Place strips of tape across the mouth of each paper cup, when making frozen pops in them, to keep the stick upright.

EGG-ACTLY WHAT YOU NEED

• Tape up a cracked or leaky egg until you're ready to use it. This is good for home damage but not for older cracks that may have occurred in the store. The bottom line here is to check your egg purchase before paying for it.

KITCHEN SAFETY

• Use a long piece of tape held at each end to blot up those small pieces of glass from the floor after a mishap.

FOOD FRESHENERS

• Write on tape and stick it to the freezer bag when storing food. Put the tape on the plastic bag while it is dry and before it is filled with labeled and dated item.

• Keep your potato chips, or the like, fresh by rolling a circle of tape—*SSO (Sticky Side Out)*—in the center of the bag to reseal. Roll the top of the bag down to the tape circle and you're done!

STAY IN CONTROL

• Put a piece of tape over the temperature control inside your refrigerator. This way, if the control gets bumped, you won't have to worry about temperatures changing and spoiling your food.

• Tape two or three pieces across gas stove knobs so they are secured to the stove top to minimize the chance of a child's turning the knobs accidently. (Just a deterrent!)

COUNTERS & CUPBOARDS

• Put a few strips of tape between your kitchen counter and your stove. This will prevent crumbs from falling into hard to clean areas. Or tape a piece of cardboard over this troublesome area.

• Place a strip or two of tape over the flat plate of your magnetic cupboard door latches if they are too tight. They will then open with ease.

• Use a piece of tape over the edge of self-adhesive paper if you are having trouble separating the paper from its backing before applying it to a shelf.

MAKING YOUR MARKER
• Make tape tabs to mark favorite recipes in your cookbooks. They wipe off better than paper markers.

• Find the beginning of a roll of plastic wrap by putting a piece of tape on your finger—*SSO*—then dabbing your finger on the edge of a roll. This makes finding the edge much easier. Use the sticky side of a short piece of tape to lift that edge!

FOR FILTER FUMBLERS
• Use a piece of tape to separate troublesome paper coffee filters. Using a 2-1/2" strip, fold one end down 1/2", apply the exposed sticky area to the top paper and lift it out. Remove tape and place it on the next paper filter so it will be ready to use as needed for the next one. Use it again and again until it's sticky power is gone, then start with a new piece of tape.

A FULFILLING IDEA
• Tape the holes closed on your salt and pepper shakers when refilling them. This way all the salt or pepper will not spill out when you turn them upside-down. This also works well when transporting shakers for a picnic.

TRASH TIPS

• Use a piece of tape about 4"-6" in length when you are out of twist-ties—or instead of—and need to secure your garbage bags closed.

• Remove the residue left on glass or plastic from a price sticker by using a piece of tape to lift it off the spot.

TO-DO LIST

• Tape your daily schedule at eye level to something in the kitchen to remind you of your plans.

• Put a piece of tape around your finger as a "to-do" reminder instead of a string. You can even write what it is you need to remember on the invisible tape if necessary.

TO MARKET

• Tape your shopping list to the handle of the grocery cart when shopping. This will allow both hands to be free and you won't keep dropping your paper.

FOR COUPON CLIPPERS

• Tape rebate coupons right to the product box, so you'll remember to use them when that item is used up.

• Remove UPC code labels from some packages by pressing a piece of tape firmly down on that area, then pulling it back up quickly. Stick it to your refund coupon as your needed proof-of-purchase.

ORGANIZE YOUR LIFE

• Use tape to secure receipts or warranties to the bottom or back of your new appliances—ones that don't get hot.

This way, if something goes wrong, you'll know right where your receipt is.

ON DISPLAY

• Use tape—*SSO*—instead of pins on backs or corners of photos when displaying them on your kitchen bulletin board. The photos will not be damaged by pinholes

• Tape the lid of a delicate piece of china or glass to its base. This will prevent it from falling off if it is accidentally bumped during cleaning and dusting.

I.D.-ING ITEMS

• Place tape over your address label and attach it securely to the bottom of your dish when providing a casserole to a church supper or when you go to a pot luck event. This way, you should get your own dish back.

• Use a strip of tape on plastic containers—especially solid color containers—on which to write down its contents or to draw a picture of the contents. It's easy to peel off the tape label when done with those contents and you wish to reuse that container again with a new tape label. You will need to use invisible tape, however, as most inks don't adhere to regular transparent tape.

• Mark the dishes and utensils used by a sick person in your home with tape so you can wash them separately.

HOME LIVING

HANGING IN THERE
• Fasten nails and hooks to the backs of wall-hangings and pictures with tape when taking them down before moving. When you are ready to re-hang them at your new residence, everything you need will be right there.

• Tape the corners of posters before tacking them to the wall. The tape makes a stronger surface and will help to prevent—or minimize—future tearing.

MIRROR, MIRROR ON THE WALL
• Place a strip of tape along the lower edge of your bathroom mirror. It may just prevent moisture from getting behind the mirror and damaging its reflective coating.

SLIPPING 'N SLIDING
• Place double-sided tape—not transparent—to the bottom of your bathroom carpeting to keep it in place.

WALLPAPERING PLUSES
• Use tape to hold the seams of wallpaper together when papering. (Test first on a small piece of wallpaper to check that the paper stands up to safe removal of the tape.) When the glue is dry, carefully remove the tape. This leaves a clean seam, minus the glue.

• Use small strips of tape at intervals to hold a wallpaper border in place temporarily while studying its permanent placement before applying paste.

• Cover your switch plates with matching wallpaper and secure paper to the back with transparent tape. Screw switch plate back in place.

REPAIRS
• Patch wallpaper tears with tape before they get out of control. Invisible tape will blend with almost any design.

A TIMELY TIP
• Tape extra batteries to the back of your wall clock, so they will be handy when they need to be replaced.

TO KEEP THE MOOD STEADY
• Wrap layers of tape around the bottom edge of a candle if it doesn't fit snugly into its candle holder.

THROUGH THE LOOKING GLASS
• Prevent sun catchers from falling off window glass by taping a circle of tape to the backside of the suction cup for extra grip.

• Tape a large "X" of transparent tape on both sides of the screen of a sliding patio door to prevent people from walking into the screen. It should give enough warning without creating an eyesore.

PICNIC MANEUVERS
• Cover an open can of pop with tape to keep the fizz in—and the bugs out!

• Place tape—*SSO*—on the underside of paper cups and plates at picnics so that strong breezes won't blow them over and away.

PROBLEM PREVENTION
• Tape the exposed metal part of the doorstop to prevent its marring a wooden door. (Don't use this remedy if you have a crawling baby or toddler who is still exploring and putting everything in his or her mouth.)

• Prevent metal wall decorations from leaving scratch marks

on painted walls by putting tape over the rough areas of the metal.

• Put a strip of tape on the wall where you frequently get many nicks, such as the wall behind a step-on trash can. This way you may not have to paint the wall as often.

• Tape the metal end of the ceiling fan pull cord to prevent its annoying clinking.

SAFETY FIRST

• Keep the fringe on oriental rugs flat by placing a long strip of tape *under* the fringe edge.

• Keep electrical cords secure and out of walkways by taping them along the baseboards.

• Place a strip of tape around a light bulb before removing it from its socket. This prevents breakage during removal and disposal.

THE ELECTRONIC AGE

VCR/DVD PLAYER PLUSES

• Tape all of your remotes together so they don't get lost in the couch cushions. A single large remote consisting of the VCR, DVD, cable and TV controls is easier to find. It also is easier to change all the batteries when the remotes are all together.

• Place invisible tape over the reflective areas on your VCR to lessen that irritating glare made by room lamps. This also works well on digital clock read-out surfaces.

TV MONSTERS?

• Tape the color adjustment control knobs on your television set in their correct position, to prevent children from accidentally changing the knob and making red or green faces on your favorite personalities

VIDEO TAPE TIPS

• To make sure your video tapes and DVDs are returned to you, label each case with your name and address (or use an address sticker) and tape over the label securely.

• Cut out the program information from your TV listing and tape it to your now-recorded video/DVD of that program. This saves the time of hand writing the label; it will be more legible and take up less room. You'll also know who is starring in the movie, it's rating and such.

• Repair video tapes that have become entangled in your VCR. Simply cut and splice pieces together with transparent tape. Trim off excess.

• Trick your VCR or camcorder into thinking the safety tab on the videotape is still there—if it isn't and you wish it was—by taping over the hole where it used to be.

RADIO RATING

• Place a piece of invisible tape over the dial face of your radio and mark it at the spots where your favorite radio stations are found. This way you'll locate them faster.

PLAY IT AGAIN, SAM

• To record over a pre-recorded audio tape, run a piece of tape across the top, covering the two square holes on the top edge of the cassette. Now you can record over it. This tricks the machine into thinking the safety tab is still there.

HOME MAINTENANCE

OUT OF REACH
- Wind tape—*SSO*—around a broom handle to collect dust and cob webs from out of the way places. This also works for cleaning the narrow tracks on sliding glass doors where dirt collects.

- Tape a circle of tape—*SSO*—to a long object, such as a yardstick, to retrieve items that have fallen behind a heavy piece of furniture or a large appliance.

ON THE MEND
- Use tape to repair a torn plastic tablecloth. It also works well on vinyl chair coverings.

- Save a shower curtain liner when a hole rips through a curtain ring. Fold a small strip of tape over the top of the liner covering the torn hole on both sides. Use a paper punch to make a hole in the tape and the liner is fixed.

- Patch cat claw tears in screens with transparent tape. The tape should hold well in any weather.

- Repair the fringe on a bedspread or pillow by winding it back and forth and taping in place. Then simply sew through the tape with your sewing machine. Remove tape when finished. Same idea works on lace tablecloths.

WEATHERWISE
- Prevent cold air from entering your home during the winter by sealing up the edges of all of your windows with tape before the cold season starts. It's not as good an insulation as professional window sealer, but it's cheaper.

- Conserve energy by taping the gauge on your home's thermostat to one temperature that you can live with. This prevents unwanted changes by others during the winter or summer months.

COPING WITH CRITTERS
- Place tape over the holes in a mailbox—the kind that is

attached to the exterior of your house. This prevents insects from building nests inside the mailbox, but you can still see if your mail has arrived.

• Patch holes in window screens with tape to keep out flies and bugs.

• Wrap tape—*SSO*—around the support of a hummingbird feeder to prevent ants from getting to the nectar.

• Pull out insect stingers from your skin after a bite by using a piece of tape. Press the tape gently over the stinger, then yank it off quickly.

• Make your own fly and pest strip using the cardboard tube from an empty roll of paper towels or toilet paper. Cover the tube with tape—*SSO*—and hang where needed.

• Pick up a line of marching insects that enter your home with a piece of tape laid right over them. It is easier than trying to pick up a trail of them with a tissue, plus it requires no harmful pesticide.

• Confounded by fleas? Here's one method to try: put on a pair of white cotton socks and walk across carpeting. The fleas will be attracted to your body warmth and adhere to the bottom of your socks. Use tape to remove the fleas and then dispose of the tape (and fleas) in small plastic bags before tossing them into the trash.

SUPER HANDY HINTS

SHOP TALK

• Put a strip of tape along the edge of the shower or tub to
  act as a guide when caulking. When you are finished, the
  tape can be easily pulled up, leaving a clean edge.

• Wrap the tip of your drill bit with tape to act as a stop marker to gauge the desired depth of the hole you are drilling.

• Hold a cracked window glass together with transparent tape until you can get it replaced.

• Tape both the inside and outside of a cracked window pane before removing it. It will hold the pieces together so the glass won't shatter, leaving treacherous glass chips to clean up afterwards.

• During woodworking, keep your seams smooth and even by using a piece of tape along the joints before you glue and clamp.

• Remove screws during household repairs and place the loose screws, nuts and bolts directly on a piece of tape. They won't get lost this way.

• Use tape—*SSO*—to remove fiberglass insulation from your clothing after working in the attic.

PAINTING POINTERS

• Place a strip of tape over your baseboard while painting the walls. It is much easier to remove the tape than to wipe the paint off the baseboard after the job is completed.

• Mark the outside of the can of paint with tape to indicate how much paint is left inside. That way you can tell at a glance without having to open the can.

• Keep paintbrush bristles in place while painting by winding a strip of tape around the bristles about an inch from the bottom of the brush edge. Dip the brush into the paint below the tape line for a smooth, non-scraggly brush.

• Attach a paper plate with tape—*SSO*—to the bottom of a paint can to catch inevitable drips.

• Cover the crystal on your wrist watch with transparent tape. This keeps the paint drips off the crystal, but allows you still to see the face of your watch. Remove tape when the paint job is done!

HOME SECURITY
• Tape a 3" piece of tape to the bottom of your doorway when you leave for the day. When you return home, if the tape is broken you will know to call police instead of entering a potentially dangerous situation.

CHAPTER TWO

GETTING PERSONAL.

— CLOTHING
— PERSONAL HYGIENE
— CHILDREN

CLOTHING

SECURE IN YOUR DRESS CODE
• Tape the front of a gapping blouse together—from the inside—under the lapel. No pin hole marks to ruin your good blouse.

- Use a circle of tape—*SSO*—to secure the two ends of a necktie together instead of wearing a tie clip.

- Keep shoulder pads in place with a piece of tape.

- Use a piece of transparent tape—*SSO*—to keep collars down and staying flat.

- Make a loop of tape—*SSO*—and stick it under the end of your belt to keep it from flopping open. This also works for keeping the tassels lying flat on loafers or moccasins.

- Knot your favorite scarf the way you like it, and then keep ends in place with—*SSO*—tape. No pin holes to damage your scarf.

- Cover shirt or blouse labels with tape so that stiff labels do not irritate the back of your neck.

CLEANING CLUE
- Remove pet hair from clothing by rolling a piece of tape—*SSO*—over the affected area.

LAUNDRY LOADS
- Prevent rust from forming on damp clothes hung to dry on metal hangers by covering the hangers with transparent tape before hanging garments on them.

- Use a piece of tape to cover and identify stains on soiled clothing before taking it to the dry cleaner.

CLOSET CLUES

• Use a piece of tape—*SSO*—to help keep slippery pants from sliding off the hanger and onto the floor of your closet. This also works well for lingerie and silky shirts and tops.

HOW SWEET IT IS

• Tape a fabric softener sheet under the bottom of a dresser drawer to add a fresh fragrance to the contents in the drawer below.

SHOE STOPPERS

• Repair frayed ends of shoelaces by wrapping tape around the laces' ends.

• Use a piece of tape to cover an area on a shoe that you don't want touched when you are polishing two-tone shoes.

• Wrapping tape around your fingers when polishing shoes will prevent polish stains on your fingers.

• Make an "X" of tape on the bottom of new, too-smooth shoes to prevent your slipping.

• Cover the leather on the high heels of women's shoes with transparent tape to prevent the leather from getting scratched.

• No stockings on and new shoes rubbing on your heels? Put a wide strip of transparent tape over your heels and you may just save yourself from getting a blister!

NYLON SAVERS

• Prevent a hole in pantyhose from getting bigger by covering it with transparent tape.

- Stop a pantyhose run by putting a small piece of tape both above and below the "run line."

- Cover the tips of your toenails with transparent tape if they are sharp enough to pierce through your stockings, running and ruining them.

PURSE PLUSES

- Cover your signature on credit cards with tape to prevent your name from smudging. Sales clerks will appreciate the clarity.

- Clean up the collected lint on the bottom of your purse easily with a loop of tape—*SSO*.

- Keep a batch of spare hair pins together in your purse by wrapping a piece of tape around them.

- Wrap the top of your house key with some tape so you can feel the correct key when there isn't enough light.

WALLET WISDOM

- Repair a torn wallet picture holder with tape. It won't show too much, and you can still see the photos.

- Tape quarters to a card in your wallet to have emergency money readily available when needed for a toll booth, parking meter or pay phone.

- Mend a cracked credit card together with tape until you receive a replacement.

JEWELRY GEMS

• Secure one end of a bracelet to your wrist with a piece of tape when putting on a hard-to-clasp-bracelet by yourself. This will hold it in place so you can bring the other end up and attach the clasp. This works for watches, too.

• Cover both sides of a fine chain with tape to keep it from becoming tangled when traveling.

• Place extra earring backs on a strip of tape to prevent their loss. They'll stay visible and accessible this way.

• Stash precious loose stones inside a drinking straw and secure both ends with tape.

• Cover the back sides of jewelry that comes in contact with your skin with tape if you are sensitive to metal.

• Wrap a piece of tape through your ring if your finger is too small for the ring to fit securely.

• Put a layer of tape around the security latch on a dress watch to prevent it from coming undone.

PERSONAL HYGIENE

STRAY HAIR
- Use tape to mark a straight line when trimming your bangs or a mustache or sideburns.

- To make ringlett curls, wrap hair around your finger and tape it into a curl. If you are going to sleep on it, use a pencil first to ensure that the curl is round, not flat.

- Attach a decorative flower (or whatever) to a barrette with a loop of tape—*SSO*.

- Use tape—*SSO*—to pick up stray hairs on clothing when trimming mustaches, sideburns or nose hairs.

- Use transparent tape behind hair combs to keep short flyaway hairs from flying around. You won't need lots of hair spray to hold them in place.

NEAT NAILS
- Put a piece of tape over your fingernails when trying on different colors of nail polish. If you don't like the color, peel the tape off, and try a new shade.

- Use tape to apply the two polishes when giving yourself a French manicure for a clean line between each color.

- Wrap your fingernails with transparent tape if you have a tendency to chew on them (it may help cure the habit).

PUTTING THE SQUEEZE ON
- Mend breaks in toothpaste tubes with transparent tape. A piece long enough to wrap around the tube several times should do the trick.

MAKEUP MAGIC
- Clean up colors in untidy multi-color eye shadow cases by blotting the surface with tape to remove the top layer of mixed powders.

- Note the color of your powder or eye shadow on a piece of tape. Even if the case becomes jumbled in your purse or worn out, you will still have the correct color information.

- Tighten the lipstick tube with a wrapped layer of tape if the cap doesn't fit properly and seems to fall off easily.

- Protect the labels on lipstick and cosmetics so that you can purchase your favorite shade again.

MEDICINAL ONE WONDERS
- Cure warts (some claim) such as a seed wart on a finger or on hands by covering them with transparent tape to "smother" the wart until it is gone. If the tape gets wet, replace it with a new piece. The idea is to keep the area around the wart completely dry.

MEDICAL COVERAGE
- Cover your prescription drug labels with transparent tape to prevent them from being smeared by their liquid contents or wet hands and thus becoming unreadable.

- Tape a packaged pill to the face of your watch so you don't forget to take it at the appropriate time.

- Use tape as one way to remove ticks from skin.

EXERCISERS
- Set the dial on your headphones and secure them with tape before you exercise so the volume and channel will remain where you want it while you work out.

STOP SMOKING: FIRST OF 12 STEPS
• Tape your cigarette pack closed with transparent tape so that each time you want to take out a cigarette, you'll be reminded to think about your choice to smoke (and whether you want to untape it).

EYEGLASS REPAIRS
• Repair your broken eyeglass frames, as a temporary measure, with transparent tape.

CHILDREN

MEASURING MILESTONES
• Place a piece of tape on the door to mark your child's height. Write the height and date on the tape. This way you won't do permanent damage to your door frame.

BABY BEAUTIFUL

• Tape down the edges of a child's bib to his or her clothes during meals so bits of food won't get under the bib.

• Tape—*SSO*—a small bow to the wispy hair of a newborn baby girl for early gender identification.

SAFETY AND CHILDPROOFING

• Put transparent tape over electrical outlets as a temporary safety measure when visiting people who don't have their homes childproofed. While this is not great protection, it may give you the added minutes needed to remove a child from what could be a dangerous situation.

• Tape *(thus "laminating")* the Poison Control phone number next to your telephone, or better yet, on each phone in the house. By the way, that number is now 1-800-222-1222.

WHEN YOU GO OUT...

• Tape a piece of paper and a pen to the phone when you leave your children with a sitter. Include the information of the place and phone number where you can be reached and any emergency numbers.

BOO-BOOS

• Secure an adhesive bandage on a child's "owie" with an additional layer of transparent tape to make sure it stays on for the whole day.

• Fashion a fake bandage out of waxed paper or gauze and tape it securely in place when your child needs a sympathy bandage and you don't want to waste a real one. Decorate it with a happy face while you're at it.

- Remove small slivers of glass that you can't otherwise reach by covering the area with a piece of tape. Gently place it on the affected area, then pull it off quickly.

- Use tape to remove the stinger from an insect bite.

MEDICAL MOMENTS
- Tape directions (written in large print) to medicine bottles so caregivers can easily read the patient's name and the correct dosage of the medication.

BATHROOM WISDOM
- Use a piece of tape to partially cover the slot in the wall-mounted toothbrush holder to prevent child-sized toothbrushes from falling through the opening.

- Tape the lock on the bathroom door back in the open position to ensure that your toddler won't accidentally become locked in.

JUNIOR I.D.
- Make I.D. cards for your kids by printing name, address, phone number, etc. on a small business-sized card. Cover the card with tape as a "laminate."

- Take your children's fingerprints by having them touch an ink pad and then rolling their fingers across a piece of transparent tape. Leave enough room to attach the tape to an index card. Date the card, label it with the child's name and file it in a safe place.

- Make an I.D. bracelet for your child out of tape and a narrow piece of paper or the back of decorative gift wrap paper. Write on it all the necessary information to identify

your child, cover both sides with tape and secure it—infor-
mation-side-down—around your child's wrist. This can
be a good security measure when traveling or even when
visiting a busy shopping mall.

TOY TIPS
• Reinforce the corners of puzzle and game boxes with
transparent tape and they'll last longer.

• Cover the speaker part of your child's noisy battery-
operated toys with tape to keep the sound down.
(Any little bit helps!)

PLAYTIME
• Teach kids how to play "Pig People" by attaching a strip
of tape to the ends of their noses and pulling it up to their
foreheads. Let them practice in front of a mirror!

• Let your children make pretend roads and streets on the
carpet with transparent tape when they're playing with
toy cars and trucks. Pick-up is easy and, at the same time,
it removes lint and dog hair from the carpet!

• Create jewelry for Barbie dolls out of transparent tape
and glitter or other bits and scraps.

• Tape two plastic coffee can lids back to back and cut a slit
through them to make an excellent playing card holder
for children who may have trouble holding cards. (This
also works for someone with arthritic fingers.)

KIDS CAMP OUT
• Tape together a teepee-shape of twigs, sticks or kindling
wood when showing a camping group how to light a fire.

- Tape a straw to the outside of a can of pop so kids on a picnic can easily find it.

- Label your child's personal items, such as hairbrushes, etc., when sending them off to camp. Cover the label with a layer of transparent tape. (Two coats of clear nail polish will give it added protection.)

- Make a nature bracelet out of a length of tape. Place it—*SSO*—around your child's wrist when going for a walk. Kids can pick up pretty flowers or leaves as they walk and stick them on to the tape while keeping their hands free.

TV TIP
- Place a piece of tape on the floor or carpeting several feet back from the front of the TV set. Tell children they should not sit in front of the line of tape while watching TV to prevent eye strain.

KID'S CLOTHES
- Get kid's clothes organized for the school week by taping the names of the days of the week on to each day's chosen outfit. This advance planning makes it easy for kids to dress themselves all week long.

- Put small pieces of tape on the backsides of metal snaps on children's clothes if the child is bothered by the metal.

- Tape an "R" for right and an "L" for left to the insides of children's shoes. This subtle guideline should help them learn to put their shoes on the correct feet.

- Cover chewing gum stuck to the soles of kid's shoes with a piece of tape to prevent their shoes from sticking to the floor or carpet until you have time to scrape it off.

HAIR BEADING
• When placing decorative beads in your child's hair, cover the end of a strand of hair with a piece of tape, slide the bead on, then peel off the tape and continue braiding.

SCHOOL DAYS
• Label your child's pencils and school supplies with his or her name, and cover it with a piece of transparent tape. A thin typeset piece from address label stickers, even if only using your last name, is a nice personalized touch. This also works well for books and notebooks.

• Encourage your child to drink his or her milk at school by filling a drinking straw with powdered chocolate and taping the ends shut. The child can take the straw along to school, remove the tape, empty its contents into his or her milk, give a stir and drink away!

• Tape important papers to the inside of a child's lunch box. You can also tape packaged cookies or such other treats to the lid of the box, so heavier items such as apples, do not crush them.

• Cover your child's lunch or milk tickets with tape in case they accidentally go through the washing machine the tickets won't be ruined and the "money" wasted. This also works for bus passes.

BROKEN BOOKS?
• Reinforce the edges of children's most loved storybooks with tape to preserve them for their many readings.

• Mend rips and tears on school books.

• Secure book jackets to their books to keep them in place.

TEACHING TIPS

• Use a piece of tape as a guide on the paper when teaching children how to write on the lines.

• Form a letter of the alphabet out of transparent tape on a piece of paper. Have kids paint over the paper, then remove the tape. The letter is revealed! This is a good way to teach letters to preschoolers.

CRAFTY IDEAS

• Wrap a piece of tape over the end of a length of yarn to make a "needle" so kids can sew through holes on paper (or plastic) plates or canvas.

• Use tape to cover the end of a marker if the top is missing to prevent the marker from drying out quickly.

• Tape all four sides of a large piece of paper or newspaper to a table or kitchen countertop to make a workspace for art or craft projects. You won't have to worry about damaging or marking up the table or countertop.

• Seal the end of a pair of scissors with tape so kids cannot cut their hair or other things around the house you don't want "trimmed."

• Cover one end of a piece of chalk with transparent tape so it is easier for kids to hold the piece. It's less messy too!

• Wrap crayons around their middles with a piece of tape to give added strength and hopefully prolong their life.

- Tape several markers or colored pencils together for children to draw multi-colored designs.

- Make items for your child's doll house out of pictures or photographs. Cover the pictures with tape, and cut the items out, right up to the edge of the object.

- Let kids make their own stickers out of anything cut from paper by applying a piece of tape—*SSO*—to the back of the chosen item.

- Connect strips of colored construction paper loops for decorative chains or as a "count-down" chain.

PARTY FUN

- Amaze your child with this neat trick: place a piece of transparent tape over an area on a blown-up balloon. Pierce with pin all the way through and remove. The balloon will not pop. Then pop the balloon in another area!

- Use a piece of transparent tape—*SSO*—when playing Pin-the-Tail-on-the-Donkey. It's safer than using pins when there are many small children at a birthday party.

- Put a piece of tape on a very young child's finger when trying to photograph him or her. It makes for some interesting facial expressions as the child tries to peel it off!

MEAL TIME TIPS

- Make an "X" on the kitchen table to indicate where you'd like your child to keep his or her drinking glass. This helps eliminate (or at least minimize) spills.

• Tape down the four corners of a paper place mat at a restaurant when eating out with young children. Pull out the crayons or colored pencils you brought along in your handbag and let your child draw on it while waiting for your order to arrive.

• Tape a paper napkin bib to a child's clothes when eating out in a restaurant and when a better bib is not available. It's easier to remember a multi-purpose roll of tape in your handbag than clips or pins. (Works well for seniors, too.)

FAIRY-AID FINDER
• Place a lost tooth on a card and cover it with tape so the Tooth Fairy can easily find it in the dark.

CHAPTER THREE

LIFESTYLES
— MINDING YOUR BUSINESS
— TRAVEL TIPS
— YOUR CAR
— PETS
— GOOD SPORTSMANSHIP

MINDING YOUR BUSINESS

MAIL STRATEGIES
- Cover your package label with tape to insure it won't come off in the mail or smudge if it is rained on.

• Snip one end of an already sealed envelope and insert the forgotten enclosure. Tape it shut. No one will be the wiser.

COMPUTER SAVVY

• Make tape "tabs" to mark computer printouts or other important pages in a document that you turn to frequently. Label "tabs" with a permanent pen.

• Attach the last sheet in a box of computer paper to the first sheet in a new box with tape so you won't have to stop to re-thread your printer when the first box is emptied.

PHOTOCOPYING FUNDAMENTALS

• Use transparent tape when cutting and pasting projects that need to be photocopied. The tape will not reproduce.

• Tape all sides of a smaller document to a larger one when photocopying to eliminate the black shadow or line that sometimes occurs along the "cut lines."

• Keep down the edges of printed pieces on the copy machine with invisible tape when creating artwork and material that has to be photocopied.

MAKING IT PERMANENT

• Change the signature on a receipt that was inadvertently signed with pencil into a permanent signature by covering the penciled signature with transparent tape.

YOUR WORK STATION

• Cover rough spots on your wooden desk with invisible tape strips to prevent snags in your clothes.

- Use tape—*SSO*—to pick up crumbs, lint and other small particles from the bottom of your desk drawer. This eliminates the need to turn it upsidedown to clean it out!

- Remove black newsprint smudges from your fingers with tape—*SSO*—when you don't have time to go wash your hands. (Or if you don't want your boss to know you were reading the classified ads!)

TYPOS—WHO ME?
- Use transparent tape to lift off mistakes from paper while typing. Place a small piece of tape over the letter or letters you don't want and either gently rub or type the "wrong" letter again. The letter should lift off much like when using correction tape.

POSTER PERFECT
- Use a long strip of tape to form an invisible straight base line when lettering a large poster.

- Lift type styles from printed matter by pressing with transparent tape, then attaching them to your project.

- Use transparent tape to lift and replace a slightly off-line letter when using letter transfers for a project.

PHONE HOME
- Cover an often-searched-for phone number in the phone book with tape, to highlight the entry. It will be easier to find the next time you need to look it up.

- Make tape "tabs" with corresponding letters to mark each alphabetical section of your phone book. You'll find it more efficient to use. (This can be a good rainy day project for children.)

• Put tape over the names and addresses of people in your personal telephone/address book who move frequently. This way, you won't have so many erasures in the book. You can write on the invisible tape easily without wearing out the page in the book.

LIBRARY BOUND

• Tape small pieces of paper into favorite books to create a place to make notes instead of writing in the margins.

• Place transparent tape on both sides of a grease spot that has accidentally gotten onto pages of books or important papers. The tape will prevent the grease from seeping on to other pages or papers.

• Repair a torn book cover with transparent tape.

THE PAPER CHASE

• Reinforce ripped holes in notebook paper (or your favorite three-ring cookbook) by taping over the holes, then re-punching them.

• Protect important documents by "laminating" them with transparent tape or tape them to your desk so they are visible and won't get lost. Just wipe them off if they get soiled.

• Put a strip of tape—*SSO*—on a podium to prevent fly away papers when giving speeches or performing ceremonies outdoors.

• Use a 2- or 3-inch strip of transparent tape to "lift" ads from the classified section of a newspaper. Press the middle of the strip of tape over the ad. Lift it gently and the newsprint will adhere to the tape. Put all of the "tape ads" on one note pad instead of wrestling with the whole newspaper. It will be much easier to organize your calls.

PHOTO FINISHES

• Tape invisible tape along the bottom edge of an instant photo to label it with the date and event.

• Create a temporary tape "tab" at the top of a small photo when pinning it up on bulletin board or wall area. When it's time to switch photos, the tape peels off easily and the photo has no damaging pin holes in it.

• Tape the negative to the back of a favorite photo before inserting it into a picture frame. If you ever want to make a copy of the picture, you won't have to search through piles of negatives to find the right one.

• Mend or reinforce torn, clear plastic photo album pages with transparent tape.

• Taping the edge of a picture frame will prevent the photo from falling or slipping out. A small circle of tape—SSO— will hold a photo to a holiday card without damage so it can later be inserted into a photo album or a picture frame.

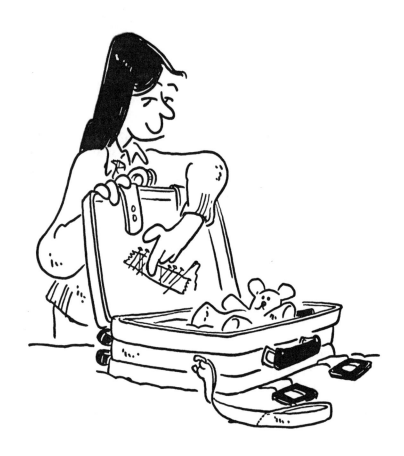

TRAVEL TIPS

TRAVEL AIDS
• Tape a threaded needle and several straight pins to the lining of your suitcase for emergency use.

• Stash a roll of tape in your suitcase when traveling. It comes in handy to mend a torn hem, wrap an emergency hostess gift or attach reminder notes. You may find more uses for it than you would expect!

DON'T LOSE IT

• Tape an address label to a walking cane in case it becomes lost when you are traveling.

• Make I.D. tags for luggage by recycling greeting cards. Write your name and address on the blank back of the card and "laminate" both sides with transparent tape. Tape these to the handles of your suitcases.

• Tape your address label to all items you simply cannot afford to lose when traveling. This enables the hotel maid or other personnel to contact you and ship your lost item home.

• Tape a pair of earrings together when traveling to prevent them from becoming separated.

TRAVEL PROOFING PROTECTION

• Put tape around medicine bottle caps before packing them to prevent (or limit) possible spills and leaks.

•Use this same technique with shampoo, hair spray and other bottles containing liquids.

• Tape a strip of floss to your toothbrush when traveling to remind yourself to floss. (Your dentist will be so pleased!)

SHOWING YOU THE WAY
• Put strips of invisible tape on the map to mark your route. You can write on the tape, noting exit numbers and such.

YOU NEVER KNOW
• Some claim that taping an aspirin in your navel will prevent seasickness on a cruise or carsickness on a road trip. We can't vouch for this tip but if all else fails, why not try it?

A HAZARD HELP FOR THE PURIST
• Do you need a reminder not to drink the water in some countries where the water may be a hazard to your health? Just tape your mouth shut when showering.

YOUR CAR

REMINDERS
- Keep a roll of tape in your car to attach notes to the dashboard. It will stick when Post-It™ notes won't.

- Tape a 3"x 5" index card with a list of today's errands to your key ring. Once in the car, remove it from your key ring and tape it to the dashboard. Check off the errands as they get done.

TEMPERATURE CONTROL
- Cover an air vent with transparent tape if you can't adjust it to keep air from blowing in your face.

PREVENTATIVE STEPS

• Place tape over car door locks before going through a car wash in cold winter months. This will prevent door locks from becoming frozen shut. Simply remove the tape later.

• Tape your automatic garage door opener on to the back side of your car's visor to prevent it from slipping down and blocking your view as you drive.

LITTLE HELPERS

• Tape coins for emergency use under your car's dashboard. Use this same idea for holding a pen in place.

• Tape the appropriate change to your dashboard for future toll stations.

• Place a piece of transparent tape on the dashboard on the side where the gas tank is located. If you drive more than one car in your family's "fleet," it will help you remember which side the tank is on when you pull into a gas station.

FOR DISPLAY ONLY

• Tape permit stickers to the inside of the car window rather than using the adhesive on the back of the sticker. The permits will be much easier to remove.

FORGET-ME-NOT

• Tape a small flag or pennant to your car's antenna with transparent tape. It will help you locate your car when you've left it in a large parking lot.

PETS

FISH FEEDING FRENZY
• Control the amount of fish food dispensed by covering half of the shaker's holes with tape.

BIRDIE CLEANUP
• Tape paper towels to the bottom of the bird cage. The tape will hold the paper towels firmly in place so the birds cannot scatter them. Droppings fall on the paper, making cleanup an easier task.

DOGGIE I.D.

• Tape your phone number to the back of your dog's collar tag. This is especially useful when you're traveling, just in case your pet gets lost.

CAT NIPPERS

• Place a long strip of tape—*SSO*—about five inches from the floor and attach it to both sides of an open doorway. It may prevent a cat from entering a room where you don't want it. Cats don't like the sticky feeling of tape against their fur or whiskers.

• Keep a cat in whatever room you choose by stretching tape across the doorway at the appropriate height. The cat won't walk through from the sticky side.

• Sprinkle ground red pepper on a strip of tape and attach it to areas where you don't want your cat to scratch. It sends an extra-strong message to a really persistent cat.

• Put tape circles—*SSO*—on places where you don't want your cat to sit—on kitchen counters, on the top of a refrigerator, and so on. A cat, no matter how determined, doesn't like that sticky feeling.

HORSE PLAY

• Wrap a layer of transparent tape over a horse's sharp-edged bridle to prevent any chance of nicks or scratches to the horse's face.

GOOD SPORTSMANSHIP

I'D RATHER BE FISHING
• Tape fish hooks to your hat or fishing reel instead of puncturing your fingers when rummaging in your tackle box for the right piece of equipment .

• Or use a small tape "tab" applied over the barbed end of each sharp hook.

• Keep a roll of transparent tape in your fishing tackle box. Ingenious lures can be fashioned out of various found items, such as string, yarn, or even some leftover bits and pieces of your lunch!

• Tape a live grasshopper with thin strips of transparent tape on to a piece of waxed paper and attach it to a fish hook. This gives the grasshopper free leg movement which attracts fish—and no hook injuries to the insect.

CAMPING COPING
• Cover match heads with a strip of tape to prevent rain from ruining the matches.

A HUNTER'S HINT
• Place a piece of transparent tape over a gun barrel to prevent snow and dirt from getting into the opening. When the gun is shot the tape will be released.

GOLF SAVINGS
• Wrap transparent tape around the base of golf tees to help prevent their splitting when hit by the golf club.

WATCH WATCHER
• Place a piece of tape over the face of your watch when in a location where the crystal could be damaged. It will protect the face but still allow you to see the time.

CHAPTER FOUR

PASTIMES
— HOBBYISTS
— GARDENING AND HOUSE PLANTS
— ARTS & CRAFTS
— SEWING

HOBBYISTS

FOR THE BIRDS!
- Create a quick bird feeder by wrapping a tree branch with transparent tape—*SSO*. Press birdseed into the tape. The birds will love you for it!

CAMERA CONCEPTS

• Put a piece of transparent tape over the flash on your camera to prevent "red eye" from occurring.

• Use a piece of transparent tape over the lens of your camera to get that fuzzy, just slightly out of focus look that is so popular, especially with portrait shots.

BINGO BATCHING

• Tape bingo cards together side by side when playing with more than one card. This prevents them from slipping and sliding.

MUSICAL METHODS

• Learn the notes on a piano by marking the keys with invisible tape. Write the letter of each key on the tape. Remove tape when no longer needed.

SHEET FEED

• Prevent sheet music from getting tattered by reinforcing the edges with transparent tape, or tape several pieces of sheet music together so that there will be no need for page turning during performances.

• Make tape "tabs" and stick them on the edges of sheet music. The tabs make it easier to turn the pages quickly and quietly when playing for an audience.

GARDENING and HOUSE PLANTS

PLANTS
• Wrap tape around the plant stems and stakes to influence the direction of their growth.

• Add support to broken plant stems by wrapping the damaged area with transparent tape. The plant will continue to grow as long as moisture can still travel up the stem. After the plant mends itself the tape can be removed.

• Attach climbing, flowering plants to trellises.

PROTECTIVE COVERINGS

• Place some tape around your fingertips before putting on gardening gloves for additional protection from dirt getting under your nails.

• Wrap your fingertips with tape before handling a cactus plant—it may prevent injury from the prickers.

SEEDLING SELECTION

• Cover any seed marker with tape to protect your writing and keep it legible during the growing season.

• Use tape and a toothpick to make "tape flags" to insert into plant and leaf cuttings. Label the tape with the plant's name and the date started.

• Label potted seedlings with a piece of paper taped securely to the pot as identification.

• Reseal unused seeds in their original packet with tape and write the current year on it for future reference.

• Sprinkle seeds on a piece of waxed paper, then take a strip of tape and place it over the seeds to make your own "seed-tape." Bury the tape in the garden and you will have straight rows growing with very little effort.

BUG BITS

- Tape pesky insects to a piece of paper and bring to a garden store or nursery for identification and (hopefully) elimination advice.

- Prevent caterpillars from crawling up the stems of garden plants by wrapping tape around the stem—*SSO*.

FINGER FIRST AID

- Pull out cactus plant prickers that are stuck in your skin with a piece of tape. Press the tape gently on the skin over the pricker, then pull it off quickly.

HOUSE PLANT HELPERS

- Use a circle of tape—*SSO*—wrapped around your hand to dust plants (live or artificial) or silk flowers.

- Tack up plant stems to a wall with transparent tape to encourage desired growth pattern inconspicuously.

CUT FLOWERS

- Encourage longer lasting cut flowers by wrapping the stems with transparent tape before arranging them in a vase. Water will continue to rise up into the blossoms if the stems aren't bent over.

- To keep flower arrangements upright in a vase, tape them together with transparent tape below the vase line and they should remain standing straight.

- Make tape criss-crosses over the open top of the vase and insert the flowers through the openings to help keep the flowers upright.

ARTS & CRAFTS

DESIGN-A-SHIRT

• Use transparent tape to bunch up a T-shirt into wads when tie-dying instead of tying the shirt in knots. Immerse the shirt in the dye, then remove tape for interesting and effortless tie-dye effects.

PAINTING POINTERS

- Paint straight lines easily when painting a craft project on fabric by taping two strips of transparent tape near each other. Apply paint in between the strips, allow paint to dry, then remove the tape, leaving a perfectly straight line.

- Apply transparent tape in different directions on a piece of paper to be painted. Brush with paint, let dry, then remove the tape. Result—a beautiful geometric design.

- Press tape in straight lines to design a picket fence when doing a watercolor painting. Paint in the background, then remove tape, leaving a perfectly straight fence.

QUILTING TIPS

- Lay batting out flat and tape it to the floor before quilting. Leave it for 24 hours and it will then remain flat, allowing for easy quilting.

- Secure a piece of transparent tape in a straight line when quilting. It provides an excellent straight edge to quilt against. Simply pull the tape off when you are finished with that quilt block.

SPINNING

- Attach a piece of tape across the width of a bobbin when spinning wool to prevent the edges from fraying or having to start over when the precious spun threads break.

KNIT ONE, PURL TOO

- For knitting machine users, put a strip of tape along the top edge of the area not being worked on when using the machine. This will prevent accidents from happening to the knitted piece. Remove the tape when ready to resume knitting by pulling downward and away.

• Place tape in a grid pattern to make a geometric design on a T-shirt project. Apply paint with a brush or sponge. Let the paint dry before removing the tape.

BEST OF BEADING

• Keep graduated beads in place when making necklaces by placing them on a long strip of tape—*SSO*—stuck to your work surface. Place the beads in the order that you want them strung, then run the string through them.

STENCILING

• Secure stencils in place on flat surfaces with transparent tape before beginning to paint.

• Use invisible tape to hold a stencil design in place when working with unfinished ceramic pieces. Remove the stencil when you're finished painting. The tape will not leave sticky residue to harm a finished glaze piece.

• Make your own art stencils by cutting designs out of cardboard and laminating the remaining board with transparent tape. The tape is easy to wipe off and can be cleaned with a bit of rubbing alcohol.

CROSS STITCHERS

• Tape the edges of a cross-stitch project to prevent fraying.

• Use transparent tape to mark off stitched areas when doing counted cross-stitch. This makes the process go along easily, so re-counting is not always necessary.

DRIED FLOWERS

• Adhere pressed flowers to bookmarks or stationery with enough pieces of tape to create a laminated surface, protecting the delicate flowers and holding them in place.

• Wrap the stems of dried flowers together with tape to help keep them in place when creating an arrangement.

• Use tape to preserve a good luck four-leaf clover that will remain intact wherever you take it.

BOOKMARKS

• Make your own bookmarks by covering a favorite picture or card with transparent tape. Personalized bookmarks make wonderful gifts.

• Make pretty bookmarks by placing tiny flowers on the sticky side of a piece of tape. Add ribbon, or other decorations, then cover with a second strip of tape.

THE GREAT FRAME-UP

• Prevent fingerprints on the glass when assembling a picture frame by making tape "handles" to hold while inserting the glass into the frame. Simply place the edge, 6" pieces of tape over the glass at several intervals and hold the glass by the tape "handles" when assembling.

STICKY SOLUTIONS

• Prevent messy drying of glue tubes or bottles by placing a piece of tape over the opening before putting on the cap.

• Use tape to keep glued items in place while the glue drys.

MEASURING UP

• Make your own measuring tape for craft projects (or to carry in your purse) by sticking two exact lengths of tape together. Mark the necessary lengths on your homemade "ruler" with a permanent marking pen.

SEWING TIPS

MACHINE TIPS
- Place a strip of transparent tape on your sewing machine as a stitching guide to keep fabric and sewing straight.

- Use tape to hold a zipper in place when making a garment. You can sew right through the tape and then remove it when you're finished.

- Keep a length of tape—*SSO*—on your sewing table to catch and hold loose straight pins.

- Use a strip of tape to hold gathers in place before and/or after basting.

- Place a piece of tape on the right side of fabric when sewing to indicate the right side from the wrong side.

- Tape a soapless, steel wool pad near your sewing machine. It makes a good "pincushion" for pins and needles while keeping them sharp at the same time.

HAND SEWING TECHNIQUES

- Roll tape—*SSO*—to dab at and remove loose threads when sewing a garment.

- Use tape instead of pins to hold down badges, patches and name tags when sewing them in place on uniforms, baseball caps, and the like.

- Use tape to secure edges of appliques when first sewing them on sweatshirts. Sew right through the tape and peel it off when you're finished sewing.

- Tape pieces of leather together instead of using pins when sewing. Pins poke unsightly holes and could ruin the expensive leather.

- Wrap your finger with transparent tape several times for protection if you cannot use a thimble.

YOUR HAND BASKET

• Line your thimble with a layer of tape if it is too large to fit your finger properly.

• Tape the end of a strand of thread to the top or bottom of the spool. No more searching for that loose end!

• Use small pieces of tape to stick thread to the bobbin when you remove it from the machine. This keeps your sewing box neat as a pin!

• Keep a roll of tape to mark new hem lengths on skirts.

BUTTON UP

• Tape pairs of buttons together before dropping them in your sewing box.

• Use tape to hold a button in place when attaching it to a garment. This works whether you're using a machine or sewing it on by hand. Remove the tape when you're finished sewing.

PATTERN SAVER

• Reinforce edges of patterns with transparent tape before sewing to provide a sturdier surface for poking pins through. The pattern can then be re-used many times.

COLOR MATCHING

• Place a sample swatch of fabric in between two pieces of tape and keep it in your purse for color matching when you are shopping.

CHAPTER FIVE

SPECIAL OCCASIONS

- — EASTER
- — HALLOWEEN
- — CHRISTMAS
- — SPECIAL TIMES

EASTER TIME

EGG IDEAS
- Apply thin tape strips in a random pattern on a hard-cooked egg before dipping it into dye. When you remove the tape you'll discover interesting patterns created by the undyed areas that were covered with tape.

• Make tape squares or other geometric shapes and follow the same method as above.

• Or just run one tape strip around the egg before dying it. When the tape is removed, the egg should have a white stripe all around its center.

• Make paper garlands of egg or bunny shapes and tape them up to decorate your home. (Don't forget you can decorate around the windows with garlands, too!)

HALLOWEEN

HALLOWEEN HAUNTINGS
• Make lollipop ghosts (or angels at Christmas) by placing a
  piece of tissue over the top of the candy, taping it around
  the neck and securing it to the stick with another piece of

tape at the "neck." You can design a tissue-covered "face" by adding eyes and a mouth drawn with markers.

• Make a special Halloween flashlight by taping a spooky design over the flashlight's glass.

• Or use markers to make "light designs" by coloring the tape strips on the flashlight glass.

• Form transparent tape into a spider web pattern to hang in a corner of the room for a spooky decoration.

CREATIVE COSTUMES
• Use tape to create a "mask" on your child's face. Kids will get a kick out of seeing their nose taped up, or squished flat, or their lips taped up or down.

• Decorate clear tape with markers and stick it on your child's face instead of costume make-up.

• Make long "witches finger nails" out of transparent tape. Complete the effect using dark red or black nail polish.

CHRISTMAS

DECK THE HALLS
• Make decorative holiday garlands out of paper and tape. Cut out appropriate holiday shapes—stars, bells, snowmen, snow flakes, or Santas—and link them together with transparent tape.

- Or just tape together loops made of green and red construction paper strips 1" wide by 5" long.

- Decorate holiday plates by taping lace or ribbons to the back of them for a festive look.

- Attach cut-out felt decorations to a mirror with a piece of tape—*SSO*.

CHRISTMAS CARD DECORATING

- Use tape to connect Christmas cards together in lengths. Decorate the ends with red bows and hang on the wall for all to enjoy

- Cut a Christmas tree out of a large piece of green poster board and put three strips of tape—*SSO*—running down the length of the tree. Stick the Christmas cards you receive on the tree—and the tape—for all to see.

WINDOW WONDERS

- Tape inside Christmas lights to the window panes instead of using hardware. This also works well when hanging garlands.

- Use tape to put up Christmas decorations on the windows of children's rooms.

TREE TRIMMING

- Let preschoolers hang their own ornaments on the Christmas tree with tape. It's safer than metal hooks.

- "String" popcorn without the string. Lay a long strip of tape—*SSO*—on your kitchen counter. Let kids place popped corn on the tape. No sharp needles needed with this technique and quicker than regular stringing. Drape the popcorn strip-strings on the tree.

• Roll a sticky wad of tape into a ball and cover it with glitter, bits of string or cotton balls to make unique decorations to hang on the tree

• Display beautiful Christmas cards on your tree, hanging them from the branches with transparent tape.

• Tape labels to the backs of your children's homemade Christmas ornaments with their names (and the date) to identify their handiwork for future reference.

• Tape colorful, individually wrapped candies together to make a candy garland to hang on the tree, mantle or wall.

GIFT WRAPPING TRICKS-OF-THE-TRADE

• Use specialty variations of transparent tape if you want the tape not to be seen. "Satin" tape becomes almost invisible when used on wrapping paper. Special double-sided tape allows you to wrap a package with no tape visible.

SPECIAL TIMES

WEDDINGS
- Tape an "X" or a line of tape on the floor where the
bridesmaids and groomsmen—and even the bride and
groom—should stand for the ceremony. The tape will not
be visible to the audience, but everyone in the bridal party
will know exactly where they should be.

LOVE LOVE LOVE
- Use tape to stick surprise love-notes in your partner's mailbox, on the car window or bathroom mirror. *Example:* "How 'bout dinner and a movie this Saturday-my treat!"

MEMORY MAKERS
- Tape notes (tucked in plastic bags) to the undersides of treasured antiques, indicating their former owners and a bit of the item's history, when readying heirlooms to be passed on to the next generation.

BRIDAL SHOWER GAME
- Use transparent tape, old newspapers and a ball of string to create bridal gowns as a party game at a bridal shower. Divide the guests into teams and give each team the same materials. Set the timer and have at it!

BABY SHOWER GIFT
- Tape a new receiving blanket around a baby shower gift instead of using gift wrapping paper. Two gifts in one!

GIFT WRAPPED GOODIES
- Make a circle of tape—*SSO*—to use on gift bows that have lost their adhesive. Works for recycling bows saved from presents you've received, too.

- Use tape to secure contents such as fruit and candy together when making your own gift baskets.

- Make "designer ribbon" for wrapping packages by covering attractive paper clipped from magazines, wallpaper or remnants of gift wrap with transparent tape. Cut the tape-covered paper into long strips to use in place of ribbon on gift packages.

Index

O

ornaments, Christmas, 89
"owie", child's, 43

P

package label, 53
paintbrush bristles, 28
painting, 2, 28, 35
patterns, sewing, 80
pencils, child's, 47
pest strip, 26
pet hair, remove, 34
phone book, 55
phone book tape tabs, 55
photos, 57
    albums, 57
    displaying, 17
    negatives, 57
photocopying, 54
piano, learning notes, 70
pick up, 55
picnic , 20
picture holder, repair, 36
pill reminder, 40
place mat, paper, 49
plants, growth 71
plastic tablecloth, repair 15
playtime, 45
Poison Control number, 43
popcorn "stringing", 88
Post-It™ note, 9
prescriptions, labels, 40
pull cord, 21
purse, cleanup, 36
puzzle/game boxes, 45

Q

quilting, tips, 75

R

radio, 23
recipes, marking, 15
recycling, gift bows, 91
refrigerator temperature, 14
reinforce notebooks, 56
remote controls, 22
ring, 37

rug fringe, 21

S

safety, 21
    electrical cords, 21
    light bulbs, 21
    rug fringes, 21
    stove knobs, 14
salt and pepper shakers, 15
scarf, 34
school supplies, 47
Scotch, brand name, 5
screens, 25
screws, loose, 28
seasickness, 60
security, 29
seeds, on tape strip, 72
seedlings, identifying, 72
sewing, badges, 79
    box, 80
    hand, 79
    patterns, 80
    table, 79
    tips, 78
    thimble, 79
shoes, 35
    kids, 46
shoulder pads, 34
shower curtain, 25
sliding door, 20
smoking, 41
special occasions, 81
spider web pattern, 86
spinning, 75
stains on clothing, 34
stenciling, 76
stingers, insect, 44
suitcase, 58
sun catchers, 20
switch plates, 19

T

tackle box, 66
tape labels, on plastic, 17
teaching writing, 48
television set, 23
thimble, 79
3M (Three M), 1-8

tie-dye, 74
to-do list, 16
toll change, 62
Tooth Fairy, 50
toothbrush holder, 44
toothpaste tubes, 39
trash, tips, 16
TV, 46
TV listings, 23
typos, 55

U

UPC codes, 16

V

VCR/DVD, 22
video tapes, 23
videotape safety tab, 23
vinyl, chair repair, 25

W

wall hangings, 18
wallpaper, borders, 19
    seams, 19
    tears, 19
warts, 40
watch crystal, 28, 66
weddings, 90
window, cracked, 28
    sealer, 25
witches finger nails, 86

Z

zipper, in place, 79

FOR A FREE CATALOG OF ALL 30+ BOOKS
by VICKI LANSKY

please call
952-544-1154
e-mail
DearVicki@aol.com

or write to:
PRACTICAL PARENTING
Dept TTP
2828 Hedberg Drive
Minnetonka, MN 55305

or go to:
www.practicalparenting.com

Vicki Lansky is the author of over 2 dozen books offering helpful household hints and parenting help. Her household hints books include:

BAKING SODA
Over 500 Fabulous, Fun and Frugal Uses
You've Probably Never Thought of
A practical compendium for one of everybody's favorite products. Learn how it works but more important, dozens of new ways to put it to good use. 120 pages. $8.95

VINEGAR
Over 400 Various, Versatile & Very Good Uses
You've Probably Never Thought of
Vinegar is more than just for salads! It's good for our health...our home...and is safe for our environment. 120 pages. $8.95

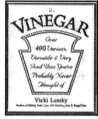

ANOTHER USE FOR...
101 Common Household Items
Wonderful "other" uses for everything from balloons to basters to hoses and hair dryers to shaving cream and widowed socks. 150 pages. $8.95

THE BAG BOOK
Over 500 Great Uses—and Reuses—for Paper, Plastic and other Bags
Learn how to make a 'bib' out of a plastic bag, turn paper grocery bags into school book covers, and so much more. 108 pages. $6.95

PLUS

TRANSPARENT TAPE
Over 350 Super, Simple and Surprising Uses
You've Probably Never Thought of. 108 pages. $8.95

Order these 5 books plus DON'T THROW THAT OUT! *$6.95* **for a total of 6 books (regularly $49.70) for only $38 plus p/h of $5.50.**

To charge a book order *(VISA, MC)* call 1-952-544-1154, or send a check with $3.50 p/h for one book; $4 p/h for 2 books and $5.50 p/h for 3 or more books to:

PRACTICAL PARENTING • 2828 Hedberg Drive• Minnetonka, MN 55305

or order on the website: www.practicalparenting.com/household.html